Table of Contents

Forward v
Chapter 1: Emotional Mindset 1
Chapter 2: Your (Business) Plan 5
Chapter 3: Business Structure 11
Chapter 4: Branding and Professionalism 15
Chapter 5: Hiring Takes Time—
    Here's How We Do it in Four Steps 21
Chapter 6: Sales and Commission
    Team Management 29
Chapter 7: Equipment 35
Chapter 8: Training is Undervalued 45
Chapter 9: Accounting and Profit 53
Chapter 10: Payroll Should Be Automated 61
Chapter 11: Marketing Like a Maniac 63
Chapter 12: Setting Up Your Shop's Workflow 71
Chapter 13: Setting Up Your Customer Workflow 77
Chapter 14: Artwork 87
Chapter 15: Pre-Production 91
Chapter 16: Post-Production 99
Chapter 17: Contract Printing 105
Chapter 18: Defining Your Own Success 111

Forward

Welcome to the first edition of *PrintHustlers Guide To: Growing a Successful Screen Printing Business.*

  I fell into screen printing because of my love for custom apparel. In college, a few friends and I began designing shirts for a local streetwear company we founded. What started as a hobby quickly turned into an all-consuming passion, and I found myself thinking about the whole process from start to finish every day—even when we weren't designing or printing shirts. Like most young entrepreneurs, I quickly became addicted to the hustle of building something I cared about and began trying out different marketing, sales, and operations strategies as a way to continue growing our budding business. As we grew, we started to hit a lot of roadblocks and had a lot of problems trying to effectively scale.

  We had purchased our own screen printing equipment in order to control our manufacturing process, but we found that we were also able to start printing for others on campus at the University of Illinois at Urbana-Champaign.

As the printing business expanded, we had to quickly learn how to handle an increasing number of artwork approvals, effectively communicate with customers, continually increase sales, hire staff and do whatever we could think of to grow a suddenly viable business.

We needed a platform we could access from anywhere—one that had an easy framework for our team to use but was flexible enough to customize for our process. Nothing existed that was simple, cloud-based and affordable. So in 2012, I started Printavo to solve these issues.

I'm so excited and proud to see where Printavo is today. Through the years, I've found that many shops run into the same problems we did. Now, Printavo helps shops around the world stay organized and optimized.

We wanted to create a guide using the lessons we've learned as former shop owners—and from working with so many unique print shops. This guide will help your business, whether small or large, to improve, standardize and grow.

We hope you enjoy it, and most importantly, find it valuable.

Keep pushing.

Bruce Ackerman
Founder, Printavo

CHAPTER 1

Emotional Mindset

Starting a business is like jumping out of an airplane without a parachute. In midair, the entrepreneur begins building a parachute and hopes it opens before hitting the ground.
—Robert Kiyosaki

Maybe your print shop started as a hobby or as a fun experiment in a garage like ours did. You find yourself looking back and remembering what printing was like when it was a one-man show.

We have found that humble beginnings are common in the print world. Rarely, you'll find a person with all the skills to run a business that decides they want to go into printing. Usually, it's the opposite: you have to learn how to run a business because you started as a printer. While it might feel more comfortable to spend the majority of your time printing, it's necessary to give special attention to running the business itself.

Are you mentally ready to jump-start your business?

Whether you've been around for fifteen years or are in your first year, your mindset is going to set the culture for your team. All eyes are on you: how should you handle mistakes, competition, wins, and losses?

Always maintain a positive and optimistic outlook, and your team will follow. Optimism is the foundation of a successful business. On your most difficult days—when sales are down, mistakes are rampant and customers are upset—the way you bounce back determines your future success.

Remember: while every shop's path to success is different, every shop owner started exactly where you are.

Finally, good physical health will make growing your business easier. Time is tight as a business owner—we understand. Take time to exercise two or three times a week, whether walking for 45 minutes or hitting the gym. Not only is it good for your physical health, but it helps keep your mind sharp and provides relief from stress and frustration. Remember that this is a marathon—not a sprint. Most businesses won't make it past their fifth year.

But you will. You're in it for the long haul.

CHAPTER 2

Your (Business) Plan

Whether you're just getting started or are looking to expand, having a realistic business plan will simplify things and provide direction for you and your team. When it comes to setting up a business plan, there are five things we urge you to consider.

What is the problem in your market?

There's a reason you're growing this business. Customers started asking you for custom apparel, and you started delivering. Dig into the pain point you're able to alleviate. Brainstorm and list what you believe your customers' biggest frustrations, fears, and worries are.

For example, a university may need t-shirts for incoming freshmen, but they may be struggling with creative design ideas, or are stuck on how to sort and distribute so many shirts. Perhaps your band needs t-shirts, and now your friend's band wants t-shirts printed as well. Maybe you want to start a clothing line, but find you are suddenly printing for your local community more than yourself.

Think through your customers' potential problems and write them down. Writing these frustrations down is going to help you understand the pain points you can actually resolve. It will define your business niche and help you understand what to focus on.

Who is your ideal customer?

Even as your business thrives, this is a question you should continually ask. It can be easy to jump at an opportunity that comes out of left field, but it could derail your core business by taking time away from serving the customers you already have. Don't print a random order on the promise of huge payments later if it means sacrificing deadlines for current customers and their orders.

When determining your ideal customer, think about the following:

- Geographic location
- Types of printing they want (screen printing, embroidery, direct to garment and more)
- Types of garments they want
- Potential business size
- Why they need your service

Now think about these ideal customers as human beings. Think outside of the scope of their business needs. Try to figure out the types of people you want to work with. Ask yourself:

- Where do they spend time?
- What publications do they read?
- How do they buy your product or service?
- Is there an age or gender bias?
- What are their priorities?
- What are their end goals?
- What makes them happy?

These questions will help you zero in on your ideal customer profile. Having this outlined makes it easier to find and market to your customers at the lowest acquisition cost.

How will you find your ideal customer?

Now that you have your ideal customer profile, it's time to establish where they can find you. Today, we're fortunate that most customers are on the internet and accessible by phone.

Many potential leads fit your ideal customer profile, and it's your job to find them at the lowest cost of acquisition. If a customer generates $1,000 in revenue for you—but you spend $2,000 on marketing and sales costs to get them in the door—your business will fail.

Think back to your ideal customer. How do they do business? Do they visit trade shows, check Yelp, search Google or ask for referrals? Analyze this thoroughly to understand their current thinking. For example: if you specialize in employee uniforms, you should get your business card to local restaurant franchise owners immediately.

Keep in mind that many ideal customers spend lots of time online, which is a low-cost way to get noticed. We will further discuss marketing tactics in Chapter 11

How will you solve their problem better than anyone else?

What is your competitive advantage? What makes you unique? Why should a customer pick you instead of your competitor?

List all the possible answers, then pick the top three. Print your choices out and keep them where you can constantly see them. Make sure your team is well-versed in why customers choose you. This is the core of your business identity—your key to delivering success.

Finally, create a customer guarantee. The ideal guarantee is backed up by a tangible penalty if you don't deliver on it. Your guarantee should drive more business and enable you to close more sales you're not winning. One example: you'll print a rush order in 24 hours, or it's free. Another is guaranteeing less than one percent printing error rate, or the job is free. Your guarantee holds you accountable and shows your ability to execute every job professionally.

How will you generate revenue?

Revenue - Target Profit - Costs = Real Profit

How will you generate revenue? What will you charge based on the services you offer? If you add enough value for your customers, you won't have to price compete—customers will pay your prices when they perceive real value.

Do not copy a competitor's pricing. You must understand your own cost structure to generate accurate profits. This will be difficult if you're just starting, but it is an iterative process that takes time to refine.

Your company's costs might surprise you as they grow. Thoroughly and conservatively consider all costs, as this will be a metric to routinely monitor. There are two types of costs in your business: fixed and variable. Fixed costs are easily estimated: rent, taxes, depreciation, salaries, and utilities. Variable costs can be more difficult to measure, like the cost of goods sold (garments), commissions, credit card fees, shipping costs, and production supplies. But variable costs are equally important to understand in order to make a profit.

CHAPTER 3

Business Structure

If you haven't formed a legal organization for your company, you need to start. It's essential for operating a business. Each state has different rules and regulations.

If you are still small, you can operate as a sole proprietor. This is risky because everything falls back on you personally—your home, your assets, and anything you own are at stake. There are elementary ways to set up a limited liability company or corporation. Visit a local law office in your hometown and weigh the different entity options. There are several ways to execute this based on the number of partners involved and how you want the business to operate.

Generally speaking, an S-corp is your best option. The company is only taxed once and your taxes are based on your personal income tax rate. You will pay yourself a salary from the business and can elect to take a year-end bonus. An S-corp also provides significant liability protection in case of legal action.

Spend the time up front to properly research how to establish your business correctly.

Once you have filed for a business license in your state, you will get a resale certificate that will help you open accounts with vendors. This is necessary to open accounts with wholesale distributors and vendors.

CHAPTER 4

Branding and Professionalism

Your brand is what people say about you after you leave the room.

—Jeff Bezos

An often overlooked element of starting a business is the image you're conveying. Branding is a major component of winning customers without physically doing work. But branding doesn't happen overnight. Your professional image is what you build over long periods of time: it's how you convey your message to customers and employees without saying a single word.

Branding is just as important as delivering quality products to your customers. Spending time on the details of your brand and maintaining professionalism will pay off tenfold.

To start, think about your company as a person. Each person has a unique voice, individual characteristics, their own attitude, and different strengths. Some people stand out, while others are harder to remember.

Here's an excellent exercise for businesses of all sizes: create a list of words that embody the type of company you want to create—and get as specific as possible. Once you have your word group, create a narrative around what your company is about. It should be summarized in a statement that's no more than a simple sentence.

"My company (your company name), is developing (your product) to help (your target customers) to solve (their problem) with (your unique trait)."

This statement should be used throughout almost every aspect of your business: hiring materials, marketing collateral, customer interactions, and even emails. Consistency and relentlessness are the bedrock of a solid brand.

Now that we have our overarching brand statement, we'll break brand execution down into three steps:

Step One: Pick Your Colors

Color usage is essential in conveying the feel of your company. Your main color should emit your brand's unique vibe. Some say certain colors elicit subliminal emotions—but don't dwell on that too much. You create the experience, the colors reinforce your brand.

Here's an example of what great branded colors might look like:

Once you select your primary color, pick a few shades that are lighter and one that's darker to complement it. Lastly: select an accent color that meshes well with your primary color, but doesn't overpower it.

Here's a great example of a complementary color palette.

These are the colors you will want to use across all customer interaction channels. Your website, email signature, social media pages, brochures, business cards, office signage—everything should utilize this color scheme. Consistency is key.

Step Two: Lock Down Your Logo

It's important that your logo looks the same across all channels. As your business evolves and changes, it's easy for your logo to be stretched out on some mediums, look different on dark backgrounds, or have changed and become outdated. Be vigilant about your logo—it is your identity.

Ensure that your logo is clear, utilizes your color scheme, and is visible on a dark background. You may want to have a white version of the logo and a black version of the logo for different purposes, but keep the size and details the same. The simpler and more identifiable your logo, the better—that way it travels well and can be quickly repurposed across different mediums.

Remember: all customer-facing materials need to have the same logo. That's how you generate brand consistency. The more consistent your logo's appearance is, the more powerful and professional your brand appears.

Step Three: Execute

Now that you've established your visual branding, it's time to implement it. Here's a list of places your logo and brand colors should appear:

–Email signature
–Website colors
–Website logo
–Facebook cover photo
–Facebook profile photo
–Instagram photo
–Twitter photo
–Invoice logo

- Box labels
- Advertisements
- Yelp profile
- Videos
- Business cards
- Company apparel
- Internal company documents

Don't skip over any items, as the consistency effect needs time to work. Tirelessly enforce the strict usage of your business logo and colors on all materials.

CHAPTER 5

Hiring Takes Time—
Here's How We Do it in Four Steps

As you begin to grow, you will find yourself needing more help. Hiring employees is a critical step for your business, and making the correct early hiring decisions pays off later. Great team members are worth much more than average ones. Poor hires are a drag on your entire business.

Here are four steps we've used to hire the right employees:

Create a great job description

Create a thorough and precise job description that contains:

- A meaningful paragraph about your company and brand
- A summary of the role: the "big picture" view of the job
- A list of job functions and day-to-day duties: the gritty details of the job
- The salary and benefits (optional)

Hunt, Hunt, Hunt

You can find great people anywhere, but it takes time. Anticipate interviewing around 30 people before finding the perfect fit for the role. After interviewing five or so applicants, you will be able to establish a baseline for the average qualities of a candidate. After many interviews, you'll be able to determine whether the candidate exceeds that baseline. You'll have an easier time knowing whether or not they're going to be a great potential hire as you develop a feel for where the candidate pool is at.

Here are a few ways to find great candidates:

- Text close relatives and friends and send them the job description
- Post on Facebook and Facebook groups
- Post on Facebook Jobs
- Email everyone you can think of that might know a great candidate
- Tap existing employees: they may know others in the industry
- Post on Indeed
- Post on Craigslist
- Post on your city's local job boards
- Post on LinkedIn & communicate with prospects
- Talk to other local print shops about their hiring practices

Your search doesn't have to stop there. If you go to a restaurant and receive incredible service, maybe that server could be a fit for your company. The approach is simple: "You know, you offered great service. I have a company and we're looking for someone. Interested in chatting?" It could spark an interview and potential hire.

Create a repeatable hiring process

Create a formal hiring process and interview your potential hires carefully. Write down a list of questions to score candidates with and save them in a spreadsheet. Here are some examples of questions we've asked:

- Do you have experience in a role like this one? Can you tell me more about your role?
- Can you tell me about your last position and what you were responsible for?
- What are you passionate about?
- What are you looking for in your next role?
- What was your salary at your last company?
- Give them an example project based on their potential role to help determine their competency.
  - For example, we might ask a production manager: "How would you organize the following tasks? What if we added three

more tasks that needed to be done that day—how would you prioritize? How do you organize your day?"
- What are your pet peeves? What makes you really excited?
- What's something you've failed at, and how did you resolve it?
- Why do you want to work here?
- Do they use the word "we" a lot? Be sure to ask what they were directly responsible for.

Hire for attitude. Train for skill.

Just like playing a sport, a coach cannot do their job if the player doesn't show up on time for practice. Consider a shadow day for potential hires. They can see if the company is a good fit for them—and you can evaluate them throughout a workday.

We also recommend having your candidate speak with a family friend. Let them know this is the next step. Reach out to someone who has interviewed candidates in the past and can provide a different perspective on your potential hire. The reason this works so well is that the candidate will let their guard down and divulge more meaningful information.

We utilize a firm called BHRS Partners, owned by Wendy Davids, who interviews our candidates after we've spoken to them.

She provides a richly detailed summary of her opinion of the candidate, which helps to weed out poor potential hires.

Lastly, bring the candidate in for an in-person interview with the top members of your team. As a group, discuss beforehand what the person is being measured on, and the types of questions that will be asked. Review their performance after the candidate leaves and go over how everyone felt. Your team can give you valuable feedback that you might not expect.

Evaluate candidates according to your goals

Your goal is to look for people who:

- Are passionate about what they do
- Went the extra mile in their last role
- Want to be part of your company
- Can speak well and handle difficult customers (especially if they are customer facing)
- Are a great cultural fit

Your goal is to find the "Wow!" employee, a person who impresses you based on how they exceed expectations because of their passion. Be prepared to make an offer quickly—and overpay if necessary. High-quality employees are truly worth a premium for the stability and performance they provide.

Hiring is a slow, purposeful and deliberate process that requires time and energy. Don't rush to get a warm body—you might regret it in a month.

CHAPTER 6

Sales and Commission Team Management

As you establish your printing company, you learn quickly that sales are the fuel keeping the lights on and your presses printing. Whether you exist in a market saturated with print shops or work in an area where you're the only shop around, you exist to fill a need in that market. Individuals, teams, social organizations and events of all types need custom printed products. But it's crucial to understand that selling a custom-decorated item is much different than selling cars, tools or copiers and fax machines.

The ideal salesperson can relate to the customer but also understands the decorating process. You may need to train your salespeople on the production process if they don't already have that background. When you decorate for a customer, that customer is in charge of ordering apparel for an upcoming group event and they have one concern—don't screw up the order! Hiring salespeople is more about building relationships than generating cold leads. Your salespeople should be solution-oriented, aiding the customer while building trust in your business so your customers have the confidence that they are ordering apparel that is exactly what they pictured.

So what's the best way to retain, compensate and incentivize a great sales team? Commissions. There are a few different ways to calculate commission percentages, but a flat percentage is not recommended. Your salespeople need to be invested in the gross margins of your product and decorating costs. It will help them sell smarter. If a salesperson sells a job that requires an eight-color flash front and back, you might dread printing it—and might even lose money on the job. If they are incentivized to reduce screens and speed up production time, you will more profitable. Then you're able to grow your business quickly.

Make sure that your commissions are designed in a way that grants salespeople the flexibility and autonomy to make decisions on the fly so they can close deals. Decorated items can turn into penny wars, so arm your salespeople with variable pricing and variable commissions. Allow them to make more commission on higher-end products that make you more money (while taking into account product cost). Margins are better on cold weather apparel like hoodies and jackets, so adjust your pricing and commission model to accommodate the seasons.

When you start working with a sales team, continually track them, teach them and inspire them. We call this the management triangle. There is no guaranteed universal way to manage salespeople, but every salesperson requires tracking, teaching, and inspiration. A regular and recurring meeting is how you can build a strong foundation. While entire team meetings can be productive, individual meetings focused on tracking, teaching and inspiration drive the best results

Tracking a salesperson means holding them accountable. We recommend you look at weekly, monthly, quarterly and yearly performances. If your salespeople use Printavo to enter in their orders, you can quickly navigate and select a window of dates to see their numbers. By tracking and holding them accountable, they are constantly reminded that they need to perform at the same level or better than they previously did. Creating these metrics is a subtle way to say you are watching and keeping a close eye on their sales while ensuring they're always on top of their own numbers. Tracking also means diving into individual jobs to see how healthy they are. Are they strong orders with good margins and simple prints? Or are they selling very tough jobs with low margins?

Teaching a salesperson or team needs to be a very personal process. Each salesperson will have a different skill set. Some might be great at building rapport, but lack screen printing acumen. They might need to see what goes into setup and teardown so they can limit the number of screens that are used in their orders. Other salespeople may need to roleplay initial calls or client visits. As the coach of your team, it's all about practice, practice, practice—regardless of their strengths or weaknesses.

Inspiring your team means being a great leader. Sales are a grind. You'll face more rejection on a daily basis than any other job, and you need the right perspective to be successful. Check in on their process and progress constantly to see how things are going. Double down on what is working. It's important that you be the leader and have a strong, positive and consistent attitude.

Remember that salespeople are the arms and legs of your business. Spend time getting to know your people on a personal level through lunches, dinners and social outings. Be their boss, but also cultivate a genuine relationship. Take care of them and show them you're interested in their success. In return, good salespeople will care about your business—and sell smarter for your company.

CHAPTER 7

Equipment

Whether you've never purchased a piece of printing equipment before, or are looking to upgrade your current equipment to expand your shop, think carefully through any equipment purchase you make for your business.

The "Why"

The first thing to think through is why you need the equipment. Are you just getting started? Or have you outgrown your current equipment? Are you ready to make the jump to automatic equipment that will increase production? Your equipment plays a significant role in the success of your business. Buy the wrong equipment and your production quality can falter. Buy too much, or more than you can handle, and you can see your profit margins spiral out of control.

Before buying equipment, speak to a professional in the industry. Spend time at a trade show, or speak to a local rep: dig into exactly why you are looking at that piece of equipment. You may not need everything that armchair experts on forums discuss just to get started. You might find better solutions for your problems than purchasing equipment—such as contract printing. Plunging into production means you are dedicating yourself to a type of manufacturing that will require much more technical proficiency than you can learn on YouTube in your spare time.

Before you buy, ask why!

The "What"

You've rationalized needing equipment. Now it's time to dive into what equipment you need. Do you have to buy brand new? Do you need to buy a 12-station auto and a dual-conveyor dryer just yet? That new direct to garment printer looks awesome, but do you know everything that goes into maintaining the beast that is a DTG printer? Buy what you need, and buy with quality and upkeep in mind.

Your equipment will need to be maintained, so it's vital that you've budgeted for maintenance expenses. Although buying used might be a great deal, the manufacturer may have stopped servicing and creating parts for that equipment. That's not to say buying used is a bad idea if you are getting started. If you are looking for manual equipment, buying used is a good deal because manual printing equipment is very simple.

Understand that when purchasing a press, your equipment list does not stop there. You will need to look at pre-press and exposure equipment. You will also need to look at the right computer printer to produce artwork for burning your screens. The list of items you'll need continues with a washout station, power washer, and screen drying rack. Approach all of your equipment purchases with this same mentality: understand the complete picture.

Here are the standard screen printing equipment needs:

1. A **powerful computer** with design software such as Adobe Illustrator, Photoshop or CorelDraw. You might also need a ripping software like SimpleSeps or AccuRIP.

2. **Film output equipment** like an Epson printer with a compatible film.

3. **Screens and emulsion.** You will need to buy a collection of screens that have different mesh counts based on what you will be printing. For finer and more precise jobs, you will need screens with a higher mesh count. A 110 or 158 screen

is a great start. You'll also need plenty of emulsion and a scoop coater to properly coat and prepare your screens.

4. **An exposure unit** that has the correct light source to burn screens. If you are going to buy a brand new auto press, look into a direct-to-screen system to burn your screens without going through film. Direct-to-screen is an advanced tool that the industry is migrating toward. Reducing exposure time is an easy way to improve overall productivity.

5. After you burn a screen, you will need a **washout station** that can quickly clean out screens and get them ready for production. Some shops couple their washout process with screen reclaiming—so you will definitely need a water source with adjustable pressure, like a low-powered electric power washer.

6. To quickly dry screens, it is best to get a **small air compressor**. Don't forget about a **drying rack** so screens can dry evenly.

7. A **screen printing press** best suited for your business volume. For manual presses, start with a four-color,

four-station press. As your business grows into higher volume jobs, an automatic press can really serve you well.

8. A **flash unit** will be required if you are printing on dark fabrics that require an underbase. Unless you plan to print solely on light fabrics, a flash unit is necessary.

9. A **dryer** that can cure apparel at the appropriate temperature is needed to produce garments at a rapid rate. Different garments and printing methods require different temperatures. The speed and heat chamber of your dryer will determine the volume at which you can print. Buy a dryer too small, and you will be backed up waiting for ink to cure.

10. Don't forget about **ink** and **squeegees**! Make sure you have done the research to buy the right ink that will print well on your garments. Different materials require different types of ink, and if you don't pay attention to this you can run into print quality issues. Squeegees are simple tools and are standard across the industry. Make sure you have squeegees of all sizes and durometer (hardness) on hand.

11. **Miscellaneous** items like **screen tape, spray adhesive, ink degrader, screen wash** and **screen opener** are small items—but are extremely important for successful production.

Overwhelmed? Don't be. There are so many useful starter packs to get you printing. The lesson here is that equipment doesn't start and stop with a press. The same exercise can be done for a heat press, a sign printer, a DTG machine or embroidery equipment. Talk to a reputable industry supplier like Ryonet, T&J Supplies or M&R to get the entire checklist before you start.

Do you really need an auto?

An automatic printing machine is one of the largest investments you will make. They can range from $10,000 to $100,000 when all is said and done. Make sure you are financially able to sustain the costs associated with an automatic press, and that you have a robust support system. Before picking the brand, do some research on the logistics involved in supporting your equipment.

If you are consistently taking orders for more than 75 pieces over the course of the entire year, an auto could be a good investment. But on the flip side, an auto can be a bad investment if you are not ready for it. There is a lot of learning involved with an automatic press, so be ready to buckle down and spend some time with your equipment. While online videos make it look easy, it is not as simple as hitting a button.

Before you take the automatic equipment plunge, spend some time researching contract printing. An automatic press increases your overhead tremendously, particularly if you are renting, leasing or financing it. You may find that contract printing is actually less overhead than owning your own equipment.

To lease or buy?

Every business is different. There is no single right or wrong philosophy to owning, buying, leasing or financing equipment. Similar to owning your own home, buying equipment may have better tax implications for your business. You may find you don't have the capital to buy. Or you may not know the fate of your business, so buying a piece of expensive equipment may be above your risk tolerance.

The best way to determine whether you can lease or buy is to closely look at your cash flow, savings, and the sustainability and growth of your business. It is not a bad idea to lease early and buy later. Independent printers are fortunate that this industry offers low start-up costs, so don't think leasing is doing a disservice to yourself. If your business is established, and you have a good track record, buying may be the answer. Either way, don't tie yourself down too tightly. Technology changes quickly.

CHAPTER 8

Training is Undervalued

You're about to board a flight from Chicago to Los Angeles. But this flight is unique because you get to choose your pilot. One is untrained, while the other has had six months of training. Which pilot do you choose? The one that's been trained, right?

Makes perfect sense doesn't it? Yet many print shop owners rush or skip training new team members because they believe there isn't enough time, or haven't developed their training method. If you don't put in the work to train your team, here's what you'll learn:

- An untrained employee is not happy. They're confused. They will underperform, and you will be frustrated because they're not doing what you want. Your new hire won't stay long and you'll have to spend time searching for another person, which will cost you time and money.

- The quality of their work will be very low. Don't believe the new hire's deliverables will be exactly what you asked for—you didn't take the time to teach them properly! You're going to have to redo most of their tasks, which costs you time and money.

- Hiring the wrong people will create unhappy customers. Your customers are your lifeblood, and well-trained employees provide better service. Unhappy customers look elsewhere, and may not return for future business with your shop.

Now that we understand the value of training team members, let's walk through how to set up your new hire training.

1. Create a PowerPoint slide deck about your company. You should include company history, your goals, the company's values, descriptions of team members' roles and responsibilities, why working at your company matters, who your target customer is, who the competition is and clearly laid-out employee expectations. Include the slides in your employee handbook as well.

2. An employee handbook is essential for any business. Include the following:

    a. Equal Employment Opportunity disclaimer
    b. Anti-harassment disclaimer

  c. Anti-retaliation disclaimer
  d. At-will nature of employment disclaimer (if applicable to your state)
  e. Pay frequency policy
  f. Benefits policy
  g. Sick leave policy
  h. Paid vacation policy
  i. The assessment process for promotions and raises
  j. Process for filing a complaint
  k. Annual office holiday closures
  l. Internal tools policy (see below for details)

3. List out all the tools you use in your print shop, including email, calendar tools and internal communication systems. For each tool, it's important to review how your shop uses it. You may think reviewing how to use Gmail is unnecessary, but it's easier to eliminate concerns down the road by providing clarity.

4. Create a company scavenger hunt with a worksheet for your new hire to complete. This will test their problem solving, communication and social skills. Provide at least 30 questions to be answered. We've created a sample scavenger hunt for you to start.

a. Where are the bathrooms located?
b. For production-related issues, who do I reach out to?
c. What's our company phone number?
d. We handle what types of decoration?
e. What's the difference between screen printing and direct-to-garment printing?
f. What's our standard turnaround time?
g. What's our rush order fee?
h. Our recommended t-shirt is what?

5. Create a detailed new hire schedule. The goal is to create a precise plan for how you will spend your time with new hires in minute-by-minute increments. Here is an example to get you started.

Time	Name	Description
9 a.m.–9:15 a.m.	Welcome	Walk through Wooden Cotton and meet everyone!
9:15 a.m.–10 a.m.	Company culture	Listen to culture presentation and learn what we value, our goals and why we do what we do.
10 a.m.–10:15 a.m.	HR	How payroll works, benefits and more.
10:15 a.m.–10:25 a.m.	Break	
10:25 a.m.–10:45 a.m.	Tools: Gmail/Calendar	Communicating via email and how we write to customers
10:45 a.m.–11 a.m.	Tools: Printavo	Shop management solution
11 a.m.–11:15 a.m.	Tools: Slack	Internal chat communication
11:15 a.m.–11:30 a.m.	Tools: Shipping	How we handle shipping
11:30 a.m.–11:45 a.m.	Tools: Phone	How we speak to customers on the phone
11:45 a.m.–noon	Break	
Noon–1 p.m.	Lunch	Group lunch
1 p.m.–1:45 p.m.	Screen printing 101	Go over how screen printing works.
1:45 p.m.–2:15 p.m.	Order process	How we process orders at Wooden Cotton.
2:15 p.m.–3 p.m.	Your role	Your responsibilities at Wooden Cotton.
3 p.m.–3:15 p.m.	Break	
3:15 p.m.–4 p.m.	Scavenger hunt	Complete our scavenger hunt worksheet.

Thanks to Wooden Cotton Print Shop for their example new hire schedule.

Here are some tips to make the new hire experience truly enjoyable:

- Purchase a blank greeting card for everyone at the shop to sign. Walk around and ask each person to write a quick note for the new hire.
- Set up your new hire's desk with necessary materials, like a computer, pens, notebook and new hire schedule.
- Give them a few shirts/hoodies with your company name on it.
- Allow them to leave early on the first day.
- Take them to lunch with management.
- Have new hires start at 10 a.m. This gives you time to start your day and catch up on what's needed before fully focusing on education.

CHAPTER 9

Accounting and Profit

Accounting

This is the portion you might already be dreading in your business: the books. It's easy to argue that accounting and bookkeeping are the most critical parts of your business. Having accurate books will ensure that you are running a clean and successful business. Get set up with a simple tool like QuickBooks or an online bookkeeping team like Bench. You will need a Certified Public Accountant (CPA) to handle reporting, as well as help you understand the necessary tax payments.

Your system for bookkeeping and paying bills needs to be the top priority. Instead of spending on a whim and doing what "feels right," having clean financials enables you to make analytical decisions that are justified by dollars and cents instead of guesswork and estimates.

Financials may seem overwhelming at first, but you can break it down into simple steps to get started.

The first essential step to clean books is to bill properly and accurately. Develop terms for your business on how you collect payments and **live by them**. Perhaps your business requires payment up front to protect cash flow or at least a down payment to cover your garment costs.

Set clear terms for collecting invoices: write out a store policy and ensure that all your customers know it. Be consistent with your terms. The key to billing is to make it simple for your customers to pay you. When you begin working with wholesalers that accept purchase orders, make sure you have a credit form on file with net terms that are clear and enforced.

One way to accomplish a frictionless payment experience for customers is to accept payments online. We highly recommend this! If credit card fees are an issue, build them into your cost so you can avoid surprise charges upon checkout. Your customers will see right through you if you do not have a set system in place for sending out bills and collecting payments. It's a good idea to send bills out twice a month, then make follow up calls twice a month on anything past due. Bad debt hurts your cash flow, so get ahead of it.

In your business, you will have fixed costs and variable costs. Fixed costs are unchanging: salaries, rent, utilities and any other costs associated with keeping your business open. Variable costs are things that change, like goods sold or anything that varies over time. Your profit margins are going to derive from your total revenue minus the sum of your variable costs and your fixed costs. This simple way of looking at your profit margin allows you to create historical data that you can reference on a month-to-month basis.

There are two basic types of accounting:

1. **Cash-based accounting:** Simpler. Your business records physical cash as it flows in and out.

2. **Accrual-based accounting:** More precise. Tracks when income and expenses are incurred or paid out.

Your accountant will go over different types of bookkeeping with you based on how you want to manage your business. Generally speaking, cash-based accounting is easier to manage and gives you a quick understanding of how much cash you truly have in your bank account. We highly recommend starting with cash-based accounting.

Keeping organized books from the beginning will pay dividends. Reduce your headaches and grant your business financial clarity down the road. Stay organized from the start.

As you grow accounts receivables (AR) and accounts payables (AP), accrual-based accounting can help give you a better understanding of your company's entire financial situation since you're accounting for payments that have yet to be made or collected. To illustrate: you might not receive payment for 30 days, even if you've completed an order for $5,000.

As your AR backlog increases, it's important to control and reduce it as much as possible. Always collect a minimum 50 percent down payment on orders (if not 100 percent). Larger clientele will often only work with your company if you bill them with "net terms"—they will essentially just mail you a check at a later date. This can be lucrative for scaling your business but also puts you in a tough spot if cash is in short supply.

As your print shop grows, reduce accounts receivables. Work hard to maintain a monthly profit margin of 10 percent after you pay your own salary.

Pricing and Profitability

Focusing on growth is contagious. Everyone wants the biggest shop with multiple automatic presses. But if you're not profitable, you're no different than a brand new printer in their basement. In fact, you'll have more issues and responsibilities as you grow: rent, employees, management, equipment, and budgeting for seasonality.

There is a popular trend in the screen printing industry to undercut a competitor's price. You can do it cheaper. You tell yourself to just get the work, and the customer will surely come back in the future. "If I don't match their price, I won't win the job." We've all thought it a million times.

Shop owners are notorious for taking on too much work "just to have the work," especially as they push hard to grow early in their company's history. On top of the burden of overwork, the owner forgoes their salary just to reinvest it into the business. "I'll take money out next month. I don't need to pay myself. I can just cut corners and offer even lower prices." This is a toxic way of thinking that results in going out of business. This short-sightedness is beginning to cannibalize the industry, but it's also a disastrous strategy; a race to the bottom. Growth is an alluring concept, but at what cost?

Have your accounts receivables ballooned out of control? Have you forgone a salary for months on end? Missing sleep and feeling like you want to just quit? It's time to reset. Start thinking about the long-term timeline of your business.

Consider this: have you ever paid more for an item or service because you enjoy working with the person that sells it? Think about your doctor, dentist, lawyer or even favorite car or clothing brand. Price is not the most important factor! Customers want a relationship. People want to reach out when it's convenient for them, get ideas for solving their latest problem, create solutions quickly and work around their schedule. Small gestures showing that you understand your customers can provide large amounts of added value. Reply to your emails within two hours, answer phone calls instantly and return voicemails the same day. Have a zero-inbox policy—when your team leaves, there must be zero emails and voicemails left in the team inbox or support desk software.

Pricing to match a competitor is the quickest way to go out of business. It's essential to truly understand your expenses. Look at what your total operating costs are per day, and lock into sales goals with your team. Don't cut corners and calculate overly conservative or unrealistic numbers.

Stay lean. Hustle hard at the peaks and spend like it's always a slow season. It's your decision. Would you rather slow down and struggle to make payroll in the dips—or be comfortably profitable with enough work to truly challenge yourself?

CHAPTER 10

Payroll Should Be Automated

Now that you have your books and staff in place, managing the livelihood of your business and team is crucial. Making sure they are paid on time and in the most professional way possible is your new job.

There are several payroll solutions that will integrate with QuickBooks, like Gusto or Intuit. We're printers, not HR executives, so when it comes to taxes and federal withholdings—leave it to the professionals.

Some bookkeepers will help process your payroll. Regardless, we highly recommend Gusto. It will create total transparency for your team about their taxes, pay dates, benefits and wages. Your accountant will love how easy it makes calculating end-of-year taxes.

As the business owner, it's your responsibility to lead well. You put your employees in a bad situation very quickly if payroll is not prompt and professional.

CHAPTER 11

Marketing Like a Maniac

You've set up your equipment, trained your employees and built a storefront. Now what? Are you as legit as a new Apple store in downtown New York City, with customers waiting to bust through the doors and order apparel?

While we all dream about that kind of devoted customer, there's no doubt that you will have to do work to develop a solid base of customers.

Before you put together a marketing plan, identify your ideal customer. It could be sports teams and local community organizations, or businesses like construction companies that need apparel for a specific niche. Define your best type of orders. Create an ideal customer profile that fits your shop's capabilities.

If you specialize in embroidery, look at professional organizations that need high-quality uniforms. It's unlikely you can cater to more than a handful of different types of people, so start by writing out a profile and creating a marketing plan specifically for you.

There are two types of marketing you should consider:

Static Marketing

Static marketing involves putting content about your business out into the world and waiting for customers to absorb it and respond. This takes the traditional form of billboards, flyers and printed advertisements with your colors, logo, and services.

Static marketing can also be done digitally through Google Adwords, social media marketing and blogging. With static marketing, you are waiting for a customer to come to you. While static marketing is useful, it should not be the only type of marketing you do.

Consider the content you are using on all channels. Do your customers actually know what screen printing or direct-to-garment printing is? It may be best to use a phrase that's simpler: try "custom t-shirts" instead. Ask someone younger to review your marketing to test if it's as simple as possible.

Here are a few static marketing examples:

- Postcards: Print 1,000 postcards detailing your business and what you do. Make sure to include your website address, email, physical address, and phone number. Include a 10 percent off coupon on the back for new customers. Distribute these everywhere you go, leaving them at tables, in coffee shops, on car windshields, grocery store boards and more.

- Live chat: Install a tool like Olark on your website for live chats.

- Business cards: Carry them around with you everywhere. Most importantly, don't be bashful about handing them out. You never know if that person knows someone that needs your business.

- Refer a friend: Tell existing customers if they refer someone else they will receive 10 percent of referred orders in cash. Email this message out to customers after they complete a job with you. Automate it using Printavo or MailChimp.

- Asking for reviews: Email customers asking for an online review, particularly if you know they had a positive experience. Positive reviews drive more business, as potential customers can compare you to your competitors quickly.

- Shirt of the month club: Create a shirt of the month for your town, advertise it everywhere you go and wear it constantly. It will take time to build a following, so be patient. This strategy can drive business for custom orders.

- Wear your company: Wear a shirt with your company's logo, name, website address, and phone number daily. Or create bumper stickers and attach one to your car. Don't forget to include exactly what you do.

- Official t-shirt sponsor: Be the official t-shirt sponsor at every event you print for. Ask for an announcement from the organizer and set up signs.

Dynamic Marketing

Dynamic marketing is the more aggressive form of marketing and involves going out and reaching customers. This can be done with printed material, but it is a much more personal experience in which cold calling may be involved.

Dynamic marketing, when done digitally and correctly, can be extremely effective. This is when you take digital content and attach different marketing tools to retarget and position yourself in front of ideal customers.

Here are a few examples of dynamic marketing:

- Local event: Host an annual event in your city. Here are some ideas:
  - Races (Marathons, 5ks, 10ks, cycling, swimming)
  - Clothing showcases. Feature the latest styles and trends with refreshments
  - Appreciation luncheons for existing customers with the opportunity to place re-orders
  - Small business appreciation day events, with speakers and refreshments geared toward fellow small business owners
  - Concerts and festivals
  - Fundraisers
  - Kids outings
- Facebook & Instagram ads
- LinkedIn: Connect with local business owners. Offer value in your initial message.
- Radio advertisements
- Knock on doors: This is time-consuming, but the personal relationship that's built lasts forever. Offer a compliment to everyone.
- Email: Collect every email address possible and communicate with a monthly newsletter. Offer value: coupons for other

businesses, tips and tricks, or showcase a few recently printed items.

- Always be selling: Actively talk to people no matter where you are. Be friendly and ask if they have uniforms, team outings or other custom printing needs. Ask for their information, then email them that night and follow up in a month. Use Boomerang (a Gmail add-on) to remind you when to follow up.

- Follow up: Continue to follow up on leads.

- Retargeting: Anyone that comes to your website will need to see your brand multiple times before buying. Set up AdRoll on your website so customers who visit it will see your brand across the internet.

CHAPTER 12

Setting Up Your Shop's Workflow

Before you fire up your presses and start decorating, make sure that you have a standardized workflow. In custom decoration, workflow refers to the stages a custom print job must pass through from start to finish. In later chapters, we'll go into detail about some best practices for workflow. When first starting out, your workflow will continuously change as more and more complexities are brought into the job. Any job will start with taking the order, creating an invoice and getting basic approval before the job begins.

Think about it this way: good information in, good product out. This front-of-house workflow will greatly influence the success and quality of your job. Once a job's art and quote is approved, products will need to be ordered, then the job will need to be proofed for production. A hiccup in the proofing process can severely delay production, so hammering out timetables with your staff and setting customer expectations with a clear schedule helps avoid any issues.

Once a job passes through the front office and artwork has been proofed, it is essentially ready for production. You'll need a separate workflow for your production team to receive the artwork and products and prepare for printing. This may vary between decoration methods, but the same attention to detail is crucial across your production department.

After a job's production is complete, the products need to travel to the customer as quickly as possible. An invoice will need to be sent to the customer to make sure payment collection and delivery goes smoothly. There are several possibilities for communication channels for invoices: mail, email, texts, phone calls, even Facebook or Whatsapp messages.

After a job is paid for and picked up, you may be tempted to think that the job is done. That's not all there is to it! End-action processes—like customer appreciation or a feedback survey—are a good way to ensure you're maintaining a high standard of customer satisfaction. Scheduling for end-action processes also creates time to handle bookkeeping tasks.

While this process may fry your brain, keeping your workflow as thorough and as simple as possible is critical. You might find that there are things that work on paper but not on the production floor. Training will be necessary, so don't be afraid to spend time with your team and make sure your process is adaptable. Don't be afraid of changing your process. Every job is unique—what works for one job might not work for another.

At the end of the day, you are building and running a **team**. Like a sports team, your business thrives when your team thrives. This industry's tight deadlines and fast turnaround times will continuously test the synergy of your team. Camaraderie and your team's attitude depend on you, the leader and captain. Spend time getting to know your team and developing a personal rapport with them. With your team, write out a plan that has S.M.A.R.T. (Specific, Measurable, Achievable, Realistic and Timely) goals so they feel invested in and accountable for their success. Plan out team meetings to discuss how things are going and stick to them. Have fun. Your team will be far more productive when they enjoy their work.

A lot of Print Hustlers got into the decorating industry because we turned our side hobby and passion into a real business. If you want to continue to expand and grow your company, you need to spend time professionally developing yourself as an entrepreneur. While you may be a talented decorator, the hands-on side of the business may prevent you from running your company well. Ask yourself if you want to run a business that decorates products—or be a decorator that happens to run a business. Developing your entrepreneurial side may mean removing yourself from the day-to-day printing grind to learn the details of running a company.

It may seem impossible. You've chosen to run a company because of the freedom of being self-employed. You're creating your own success—that means growing your knowledge and having experiences you've never had before.

Now get out there and hustle!

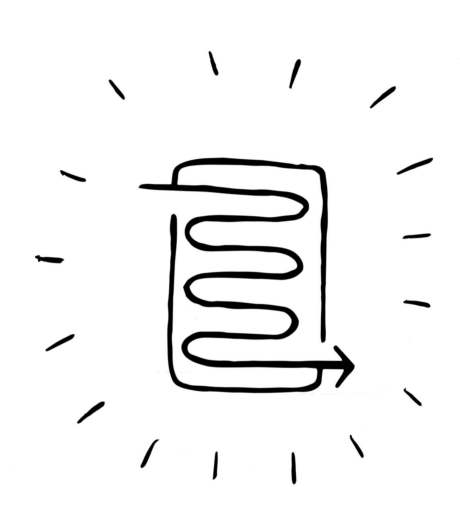

CHAPTER 13

Setting Up Your Customer Workflow

So your shop is open for business and ready to accept orders. Implementing a simple, repeatable process for building orders is how you fulfill jobs quickly—and make money! This short chapter will demonstrate how to best build and execute new orders, talk about how to get orders moving and provide relevant information for how to quote jobs.

Before you get started, there's one important thing to remember about quotes: it's *not* an estimate. Once a customer approves a quote, it is a legally binding cost that the customer has agreed to pay. This makes quoting your work correctly critical to the success of your business.

When a customer first approaches your business with a request for service, you'll need to gather a standard set of information that will allow you to take the job to completion. You want as little back and forth with the customer as possible. As the shop's owner, it's your responsibility to collect all of the information you need to complete the job correctly and on time. Make this process as easy as possible for your customer.

Finding the balance between too much and too little information is how to avoid waste and confusion. Getting the info you need the first time eliminates the need for additional follow-ups and miscommunication.

Here are 12 crucial pieces of information that you'll need from each customer. We've broken them down into customer information and order information:

- **Customer Information**
  - Name
  - Billing and shipping address
  - Phone number
  - Additional contact person(s)
  - Budget

- **Order Information**
  - Shipping address (are there multiple shipping addresses?)
  - Due date
  - What type of printing (two-color, one-color, embroidery, etc.)
  - Item type (Gildan 2000 Red, Allmade 200 Tri-Blend, etc.)
  - Color

- Quantities and sizes
- Artwork (provided by the customer or the shop)
- Special order info (split shipments, name spellings, unique terms and conditions, etc.)

It may seem uncomfortable asking a person to name their budget, but it gives you an opportunity to showcase your expertise as a printmaker. If a customer has a $200 budget but wants to order 500 shirts with a two-color front and back print, you can save everyone a lot of time and offer more realistic options up front. Be clear on whether the customer is going to provide artwork versus expecting you to provide proofs from a concept. That will allow you to plan and schedule art prep for your production team and give your customer a realistic timeline for the job's completion.

After verifying the customer's information, you're ready to write your quote. The first step:

Date the job: You've gotten a due date from a customer, but it's essential for your team to be clear on two dates: the agreed-upon customer due date *and* the production date. Distinguishing between the date when the customer expects the goods in-hand and the production date provides control. It can also give you the freedom to reschedule and prioritize orders as production needs change, preventing you from losing business because of a scheduling mix-up—or needing to rush to get something done at the very last minute.

In Printavo, we built an easy way to set a customer due date and a production due date separately. The production due date is what we display on your shop's calendar and production notes.

After planning out production dates, the next part of writing your quote is:

Inform the job's details: This step consists of giving your order a name that communicates what this job holds, as well as any special order information. Shops lose customers because they fail to track specific or special requests. It only takes one slip up for a customer to decide to take their money elsewhere. Sometimes this mishap can involve a split shipment, unique terms and conditions, or even just the spelling of a name. There are plenty of other legitimate reasons to lose customers, so don't make misplacing or losing information a problem for the people you print for.

It's important to have a name for your job and a designated place to house special order information. Customers appreciate the assurance of seeing that you're keeping track of their requests, and your team will be grateful to have all that information at their fingertips.

You want fields in your job quotes like this:

At Printavo, we add these features on every customer's quote to make sure you don't miss anything:

- **Nickname** is the title of the order that shows on your calendar.
- **Notes** are where you put customer-facing notes. These include special terms and conditions, shipping instructions and unique order requests.

- **Production notes** are for any internal-facing notes between your team. This creates a centralized channel for production communication. It's all right in front of your team, attached to the quote and viewable only by staff.

The next element to building out a successful quote is adding in the items, quantities and prices.

Adding items and pricing: There are five main pieces that every line item on your quotes and invoices should have:

- Type/Category
  - Screen print
  - Embroidery
  - Vinyl
  - Promotional
  - Other types of decoration
- Item SKU
- Description
- Sizes (optional)
- Item quantity totals
- Price

When all is said and done, each of the line items on your job quotes should look something like this:

All that's left to do is:

Attach your artwork*: The final step to a successful quote is adding your artwork. Whether it is customer provided, stock art, or designed by you—get it attached to your quote and approved by the customer so you can print and get paid.

If you're attaching artwork, consider the file size and file type of the art you're sending to the customer. If your file that requires software like Adobe Photoshop or Illustrator but the customer doesn't have that software, they can't see it. This is unprofessional and reflects poorly on your business. Or, just as bad, an image gets sent that is too small for the customer to see clearly. It may be beautiful art, but when the customer can't see it you're left looking unprofessional. This is another one of those unique industry challenges. When quoting a job out in Printavo, we've tried to eliminate this obstacle by allowing you to attach as many different file types as you want to each line item. It's easy to allow your customer to see large, full-resolution files and photos.

If you're not using a tool like Printavo, you'll want to be sure to attach a common file type like PDF or JPEG. Use a high enough resolution to give your customer a clear view of the art that will be on their order. You may even want to go one step further and give them a mock-up of the garment along with the artwork. The clearer the completed picture of their product, the better.

*There are quite a few things to keep in mind when approaching artwork approval with customers. First, this step is where most breakdowns occur. There is a lot of potential for back and forth over ideas, leading to miscommunication and mismanaged expectations. Second, you may receive artwork from a customer that is under no circumstances acceptable for you to print. This often creates a need for adjustment, which can elicit pushback from customers and potential frustrations for artists. Finally, you'll need to decide if you're going to charge an extra fee for designing or consulting on the artwork. It's important to communicate this up front, so your customer isn't surprised by what they think are hidden fees. Take a look at our chapter on artwork to get more in-depth practices on how to best navigate these challenges.

After attaching your artwork, your quote is ready for approval. Save it and send it to your customer.

CHAPTER 14

Artwork

One of the best parts of running a business is working with so many different types of people. Ironically, this is a very challenging part as well. In our shop, it always seemed like the art proof and approval process brought out the most frustration. The back-and-forth discussions, constant miscommunications and unclear expectations created a hotbed of problems preventing us from growing our business. Finding the simplest way to execute approvals became an immediate priority.

The one guiding principle that we found to be crucial to our success? Thoughtfully create a repeatable process.

The way you attach your quote and send your art proof to the customer—and the verbiage you use to communicate expectations—will set the tone for how positive or negative the complicated art approval process becomes.

Your process should look something like this:

1. Initiate artwork request. This can be customer-provided, based on a customer's inspiration, or a custom design you offer during the quoting process.
    a. If the art is customer provided, make sure you *communicate clearly about image quality requirements.*
    b. If the art is custom designed, then the customer's inspiration can be requested during quoting.
2. Complete artwork
    a. This can be done through a number of programs and depends on the type of job you're printing. Common programs are CorelDraw or Adobe Illustrator.
3. Proof sent to the customer via email or quoting software*
4. Proof approved or denied by customer
5. Proof finalized or revised (if changes are made, communicate and refine until approved)
6. Proof attached to order and sent to production.

Going back and forth with a customer about artwork revisions can be arduous—especially if you have multiple orders in progress at the same time (perhaps with the same customer!) and still need to move the rest of your orders forward. Having a streamlined system in place helps communication and eliminates potential confusion. It also ensures your art approval process doesn't hold your production line hostage. Create a coherent process for art revisions to reduce wasted time.

*In Printavo, we've created a messaging system that's accessible on every quote to host all of an order's details and communications. This reduces confusion about orders.

    Edit   Overview   Payments/Expenses   Messages   Tasks

If you're looking to take your approval process to the next level of efficiency, we have three words: preset email templates. The approval process is essentially the same for every customer, so preset email templates can save you lots of time. Consider how many of the same emails you send each month. You can store these emails on a living document in your server or inside your quoting program and change them as needed.

CHAPTER 15

Pre-Production

Now that we are through the basics of order intake, we can begin looking at your company's pre-production workflow. Ask yourself these two questions:

1. What am I offering to my customers?
2. How can I create a system for seamless, cost-effective and efficient production?

After reading through this guide, you will be able to map out the basic steps of pre-production.

Pre-production is one of the most critical processes of any print job. If your pre-production setup is done correctly, the job will run seamlessly all the way through completion. Most preventable mistakes happen during pre-production—costing you lots of money. Spending time now to refine pre-production processes acts like an investment: you reduce the amount of money and time you have to spend later. Plus, we've already done the heavy lifting for you!

First, let's talk mistakes. What are the two main reasons mistakes happen? The production process is broken, or a team member misunderstands the process. It is up to you to create a process that eliminates mistakes—and then *train your people* to follow your process properly.

Tips for developing a rock-solid pre-production process:

- Avoid abbreviations: they create errors and confusion.
- Iterate your process: revisit your process monthly or quarterly. Sit with your team to hear how they would improve their part of your process.
- Create a list of tasks employees should NOT do: keep them focused on specific tasks that pertain to their role.

Implementing an effective pre-production system requires thorough training for all of your shop employees. We all want our shop to be operating at full efficiency, like a well-led boat rowing toward the Port of Profit. If your team is rowing at different speeds and in different directions, your boat goes nowhere. You want zero friction between your team and your process. Create predetermined, agreed-upon roles for pre-production. This allows you to train your team effectively—and to hold your employees accountable. Keep everyone rowing at the same speed toward the same goal!

This list will cover pre-production procedures for screen printing, embroidery and sign printing (while assuming your initial artwork and quote has been approved). Every workflow is going to vary from shop to shop—and that's okay. Spend time writing out what works best for *your* workflow, making sure to add specific team members by name or department. Pre-production is where the most costly and time-consuming mistakes are made in this industry: be extremely thorough.

Manually plot out your workflow. The first step in developing a pre-production process is creating a workflow. Here's the foundation of our own pre-production workflow:

- **Screen printing:**
  - Proof the artwork
  - Request approval of your mockup or proof
  - Finalize the artwork & plan screens (if rejected, revise until approved)
  - Order goods from vendors
  - Receive and check-in goods

- Print films
- Send films to production
- Check-in films
- Burn screens

- **Embroidery:**
  - Proof the artwork
  - Request approval of your mockup or proof
  - Finalize artwork (if rejected, revise until approved)
  - Order goods from vendors
  - Receive and check-in goods
  - Digitize artwork
  - Sew out a sample for approval

- **Signs/Banners:**
  - Proof the artwork
  - Request approval of your mockup or proof
  - Finalize artwork (if rejected, revise until approved)
  - Set media

By developing color-coded status updates, we've designed a production process that allows us to completely customize, manage and control the workflow. We eliminated guesswork around where exactly an order is, reducing missed steps in the production process. Here's how one shop set up their color-coded workflow in Printavo:

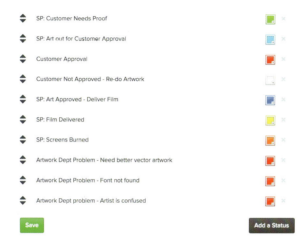

Notice that these are progressive stages of the job status—not individual tasks.

Develop and assign specific tasks for each step. After you have created your initial workflow, break down the individual tasks required for each step and assign these to specific team members. You'll have measurable expectations—and ensure each team member understands their exact role in the process.

Introduce standardized communication practices. Once your order statuses, workflow and individual tasks are assigned, set up a standard communication system. Whether it's emails or in-office messaging, establish exactly how and when information is passed along the chain. Then your team knows the specifics about how and when to expect information.

In a short amount of time, you've created your pre-production process: job statuses, specific tasks for specific people, and a clear route for communication. Your shop is ready to start rowing. Let's go!

CHAPTER 16

Post-Production

Make your customer's final impression your best impression.

After you complete the printing and decoration process, you have to finish strong. You've worked hard to successfully produce your product, so you need to create a system for follow-through during post-production. Post-production serves a few powerful purposes. It assures that your customer receives exactly what they ordered, and it guarantees they get their order in a timely fashion. The most compelling reason for a strong post-production process? It creates very satisfied customers that return over and over to do business with you. They'll even refer your business to their network.

Your post-production process must ensure that your production staff has completed the job and decorated the goods according to your shop's standards. But most importantly, you must meet your customer's requirements. These final steps are the quality control aspect of the manufacturing process. Include your quality control checklist with every single work order for every job.

Here's an example of a quality control checklist:

- Every print is correctly applied.
  - Correct garment side
  - Correct colors
  - Correct print locations
- Any erroneous ink spots are removed with a spot remover tool.
- All items are accounted for and exactly match the work order.
  - For smaller shops that can't add extra employees, have your printers complete this step. It holds printers accountable for the accuracy of their work.
- Ensure all shipping details are clear and accurate. Your shop might ship jobs or allow for customer pick up at a retail location. Customer due dates are sensitive, so tailor your post-production to your customers' schedules and needs.

Once you've printed a perfect job, have your staff carefully package and fold your items properly. Do not use boxes that are too large. Use the least amount of packaging necessary.

Here's a quick and actionable guide to quality control and packaging:

1. Make sure that garment sizes are stacked together and boxed for the customer in a way that will make unboxing easy. If your shop counts items in front of your customer before pick up, find a way to count the garments quickly when the customer arrives.
2. Always label your boxes. If your shop does not have custom boxes printed, consider printing packing stickers for simple labeling.
3. Create a portion on your box that shows the total box count (ex: 1 of 5). Label your boxes by size and job name so that all your boxes are accounted for during shipping and pick-up.
4. Initial each box. It holds you accountable and your customers can see that you took extra precautions to double-check the order.
5. Print out packing slips and apply them to a box using packing list envelopes.

You're almost there! Time to finish the job. Print your shipping labels. A solution like EasyPost, that prints professional and cost-effective labels, is valuable when you're shipping lots of items. Follow through at the end of the job by communicating with the customer multiple ways once you have printed your shipping labels and their items are ready for pick up. An email is a decent preliminary step, but a personal phone call adds an extra layer of customer satisfaction. Call to let the customer know their newly printed custom goods are ready. After you have called them, send a follow-up email with tracking info, as well as the receipt. If applicable, send your invoice as well. Be sure to clearly outline your payment terms so your customer is not surprised with your requirements.

Every shop will be slightly different. The key here? Write out a plan and implement it. Then, continue to perfect it over time based on how your business responds. While most owners might think post-production ends once the goods are out the door, you can take several measures after a job is finished to create a loyal customer. After the job goes well, ask them to leave you a review on Google, Yelp, Facebook and your social media pages. Send a follow up after their event to see how the shirts turned out—and *always* continue selling. Let them know about their next order way before they know they need it—and show them how simple you will make the entire process for them.

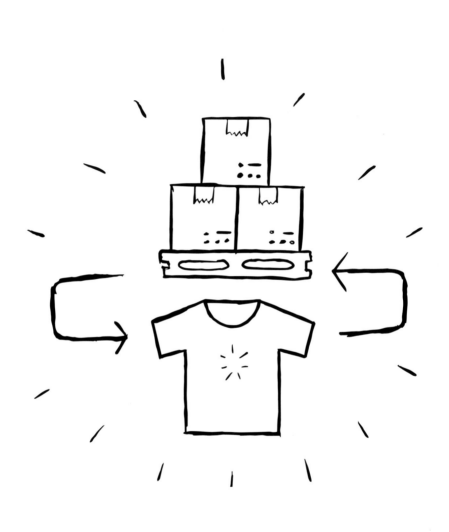

CHAPTER 17

Contract Printing

New to the printing industry? Contract printing might be a foreign concept. But it can be something you rely on to launch your business. Contract printing is a business-to-business practice where the customer shop supplies the raw products and print-ready artwork to the contract printer. The contract printer decorates the products and returns them to the customer shop. In this chapter, we will discuss the pros and cons of contract printing. We will cover the basics of contract printing, and also detail steps to take if you want to become a contract printer.

Contract printers are often set up with multiple presses and decorate on anything you send. When your business cannot personally produce the volume of orders that you are taking, start exploring relationships with contract printers. Perhaps you have not purchased your first auto yet, and you get a rather large order you don't want to turn down. This is where contract printing shines. You might not have the equipment required to decorate your orders. You don't do sublimation, direct to garment or even embroidery, so—you *contract it out*. This practice has allowed for custom apparel companies that do not print a single thing in-house and rely solely on contract printing!

Find the *right* contract printer. While most printers may claim they *are* contract printers, do some research to find the best ones. After all, your brand name is still selling the apparel, so you want to make sure you meet your customers' standards. Start by asking your local sales reps: your apparel rep, ink rep and equipment rep are great resources. They will be able to point you in the right direction to generate a good relationship with a professional contract printer.

After you find trusted printers, make sure you closely communicate about their service and understand their exact terms. You want to understand print costs per impression since every shop will have slightly different pricing. They should offer you a term sheet that outlines quantities and price breakdowns. Contract printers usually have strict turnaround times, typically with an upfront breakdown of their exact schedule. You will also have to consider any additional fees. Many contract printers charge premiums for set-up costs, additional screens, special inks and even artwork-related fees like digitizing costs. For an additional fee, some contract printers even offer individual bagging, special tagging and unique labeling for your apparel. Take all these fees into account when pricing contract printed items to your customers.

When you are comfortable with your contract printer, ask them how they like to receive their orders. Most will prefer that you send a work order, packing slip, print-ready artwork and a purchase order for them to use. In Printavo, you can send your contract printers a direct link so they can see all of the job's specific information. You can also upload artwork to the job online so the contract printer can easily download it. When you have a strong relationship with a contract printer, you can make them a user in your Printavo system so they'll be notified whenever you take an order.

 The contract printer will deal with your shop in much the same way you deal with customers: through art proofs and payment requests. When you contract with a print shop for a long time, consider asking for better pricing once you've both benefited from your relationship.

One downfall to using a contract printer? You are putting the decoration of your products in another company's hands. This seems like a very easy solution. So recognize that they have a margin of error in their printing that they are not ultimately responsible for. If an item does not come correctly printed, it's tough to rectify the situation in a timely fashion for your customers. As always, mistakes do happen in this industry, so be prepared and always have a backup plan. Contract printing can also have heavy reordering fees, as they make much of their profits from set-up and impression premiums.

CHAPTER 18

Defining Your Own Success

Why are you doing this all of this? Financial freedom? Happiness? Why did you pick up this book and read it? These are the pressing questions you must ask yourself before starting. You have decided to start your own business and therefore you have to *define your own success*.

Success and happiness look different for everyone. Define what success is to you. Realize that the shop next door will not determine your success, because you create your own success.

Think through the *"Why?"* behind your business. Do you want to make your own hours and enjoy time with your family? Maybe you worked for someone else and did not like the money they paid you. Are you passionate about the arts and want a profitable way to express yourself? Some people believe success has a dollar sign attached to it. That is a dangerous definition of success. Money alone will not make happiness. There's no salary great enough to overpower the joy of self-actualization.

Write down your short-term business goals. Follow those with your long-term business goals. Then write down your wildest dreams for your business. Paint a detailed picture of how your business will run, act and operate. Imagine how many employees you'll have, what your facility looks like and how much your community will love your work. Your goal doesn't need to be running a shop with 20 automatic presses firing at full speed. That might not make you happy (imagine the stress and problems!) or even successful. Be true to *your* goals.

Imagine the life you want to live five, ten or even twenty years from now. What does that mean for yourself, your family and your well-being? Where do you want to live, and what kind of work-life balance do *you* want to have? The bigger you make your business, the harder it will be to create the balance you want in your life. No one wants to work forever. Make your roadmap for how you'll get there.

Soon, you may be so inundated with your business that success becomes extremely difficult to taste and feel. To feel successful in the long-term, you have to do the short-term work to consistently measure and model where you are and how to improve. Leverage the power of friends, trusted advisors, business partners, industry associates, local experts, business mentors and even your customers for guidance along the way. You are never alone in anything you do.

Making steady and stable progress toward fulfilling *your* plan for success will directly correlate with your sense of happiness. Don't forget that the most powerful feelings of happiness come from the feeling that you have made your vision of success a reality. As you finish our book, we want to leave you with this final message for how to grow and succeed: push hard to make your business exactly what *you* want it to be.